TRACTORS
at Work

D. R. Addison

PowerKiDS
press

New York

For my little truck experts, Deming, Riley, and Hannah

Published in 2009 by The Rosen Publishing Group, Inc.
29 East 21st Street, New York, NY 10010

First Edition

Editor: Joanne Randolph
Book Design: Greg Tucker
Photo Researcher: Jessica Gerweck

Photo Credits: All photos Shutterstock.com.

Library of Congress Cataloging-in-Publication Data

Addison, D. R.
  Tractors at work / D.R. Addison. — 1st ed.
     p. cm. — (Big trucks)
  Includes bibliographical references and index.
  ISBN 978-1-4358-2704-2 (library binding) — ISBN 978-1-4358-3090-5 (pbk.)
ISBN 978-1-4358-3096-7 (6-pack)
  1. Farm tractors—Juvenile literature. 2. Truck tractors—Juvenile literature. 3. Earthmoving machinery—Juvenile litertaure. I. Title.
  TL233.15.A33 2009
  629.225'2—dc22
                                          2008024300

Manufactured in the United States of America

Contents

Here comes a tractor. It is ready to work.

Some tractors are big. This big tractor works on a farm.

Some tractors are small. This small tractor is working on a farm, too.

Some tractors have arms on them. These arms can have tools fixed to them.

Tools help tractors do different jobs. This tractor pulls a **trailer**.

This tractor has a **plow** fixed to it. It uses the plow to dig holes for seeds.

15

This tractor **sprays** the plants with food. This food will help the plants grow.

This tractor has a roller fixed to it. The roller helps even out earth on the farm.

Some tractors are used at **construction sites**. This tractor has a shovel and digger on it.

Even toy tractors work hard every day. Good job, tractors!

Words to Know

construction site

plow

sprays

trailer

Index

Web Sites

Due to the changing nature of Internet links, PowerKids Press has developed an online list of Web sites related to the subject of this book. This site is updated regularly. Please use this link to access the list:

www.powerkidslinks.com/bigt/tractor/